MEDITATIONS

An Hachette UK Company
www.hachette.co.uk

Material first published in *The Meditation Bible* in Great Britain
in 2005 by Godsfield Press,
a division of Octopus Publishing Group Ltd
Carmelite House, 50 Victoria Embankment, London EC4Y 0DZ
www.octopusbooks.co.uk

This edition published in 2017 by Bounty Books, a division of
Octopus Publishing Group Ltd

ISBN 978-0-7537-3265-6

A CIP catalogue record for this book is available from the
British Library

Printed and bound in China

10 9 8 7 6 5 4 3 2 1

For the Bounty edition
Publisher: Lucy Pessell
Designer: Lisa Layton
Editor: Sarah Vaughan
Production Controller: Beata Kibil

MEDITATIONS

*For mindfulness,
healing and stress relief*

MEDITATIONS

*For mindfulness,
healing and stress relief*

CONTENTS

INTRODUCTION

If you are new to meditation, you will feel comfortable with this book. And if you are an experienced meditator, you may find renewed inspiration here.

Whether you are a beginner or have been meditating for some time, this book offers a broad collection of simple, effective meditations for enriching your daily life and deepening your spiritual practice. All are clearly explained, with easy-to-follow instructions to help you.

WHY MEDITATE?

Meditation has been practised in many cultures for thousands of years because its benefits are numerous. In all areas – physical, mental, emotional, psychological and spiritual – meditation has the potential to help you create a better life.

• Meditate for better health – Simply meditating on your breath can lower your blood pressure, slow your heart rate and ease anxiety. Meditation can also help you heal from illness, manage pain and prevent illness.

• Meditate to sharpen your mind – You can bring your new found mental skill and discipline to your work and family life, making you a more effective boss, worker, spouse or parent.

• Meditate to be more aware of your body and mind – Improve your concentration and feel less overloaded with life.

• Meditate to balance your emotions – Stay conscious of your emotions, and help create mental peace and less emotional reactivity. Some of the meditations provided here help you to transform negative emotions into positive ones.

• Meditate to heal psychological problems – If you have suffered from addictions, unresolved grief, childhood neglect or trauma or other psychological issues, meditation is a wonderful way to support yourself during the healing process.

• Meditate to contemplate the mysteries of life – If you feel bogged down in the materialistic view of the world that pervades our culture, meditate to transform and transcend it.

• Meditate if you want to understand the meaning of your life, your destiny, your connectedness to all living beings and the sacredness of reality.

WHAT IS MEDITATION?

You may think that meditation is an exotic practice which is connected with Eastern religions. Or you may think it has something to do with a special sitting posture. You may also think it has to do with being 'holy'.

None of the above is true. Meditation is simply making a choice to focus your mind on something. In fact, reading a book is a form of meditation, as is watching a movie or advertising on TV.

Practise for a happier life Meditation is not mystical, otherworldly or inaccessible. It is not reserved for the 'elite' nor those steeped in knowledge of Eastern or alternative religions. Meditation is very down-to-earth and practical and it is available to everyone.

Although many of the meditations in this book are inspired by ancient and modern spiritual traditions, none requires faith or belief. If you have no spiritual practice, or do not believe in a god or higher power, try these meditations with the motivation of simply creating a happier life for yourself. You can meditate by creating special time consciously to focus your mind in positive and helpful ways, but it helps to have some direction and guidance as to how to do this.

This book provides a variety of meditations to get you started.

HOW TO START

• Start with an open mind. If you are new to meditation, you may find your views challenged by some of the exercises. If you are an experienced meditator, you may find the meditations are different from those you are used to.

• Be willing to let meditation change you. Even if it is positive, change can be scary. But the benefits far outweigh the temporary discomfort that comes with change.

• Develop a consistent practice, daily if possible. The ritual of sitting down at the same time and in the same place every day will help make meditation a part of your life.

• In the beginning you may want to sample meditations from each of the eight sections. While in the exploration stage, feel free to meditate at different times of the day. But try to meditate once a day, regardless of the time or place.

• After you have explored the different forms, you may find one or two you want to stay with on a long-term basis. At this point, settle on a time and place that is consistent day to day.

• The changes, realizations and benefits of meditation accumulate over time. There is no quick fix or instant enlightenment. That is not to say that meditation will not feel good right away, but regular practice will reap bigger rewards.

• In the beginning, you may have trouble staying with a daily discipline due to the pressures of life. But committing to a daily practice is the best way to approach meditation.

• Your consistency will sustain you through periods of laziness, busyness or unhappiness with the speed of your progress.

CALMING & CENTRING

WATCHING YOUR BREATH

This is one of the simplest of all meditations, yet one
of the most powerful and rewarding.

Meditating on the breath each day provides a
foundation for all other forms of meditation.

Meditate daily, morning and evening, for ten minutes at a time. Build up gradually to longer sessions.

1 Sit cross-legged on a cushion with your bottom slightly raised. If you can't sit cross-legged, sit on a chair.

Keep your back straight, your shoulders level and relaxed and your chin parallel to the floor. Lower your eyes and focus about a metre (three feet) in front of you. Rest your hands gently on your knees.

2 Breathe normally through your nose, using your abdomen rather than your chest. Check your posture and relax any part of your body that is tense.

3 Begin counting your breath on each exhalation; when you reach ten, begin again. Thoughts will intervene and when they do, simply let them go and return to counting your breath.

4 After ten minutes or so, end your session. Try to bring focus and concentration into your daily life.

THOUGHT CLOUDS

Thoughts inevitably arise when you meditate on
your breath.

Labelling your thoughts as they emerge will help you
to refocus on your breath and calm your mind.

Try this variation on breath meditation for ten minutes at a time, morning and evening.

1 Sit cross-legged on a cushion with your bottom slightly raised. If you can't sit cross-legged, sit on a chair.

Keep your back straight, your shoulders level and relaxed and your chin parallel to the floor.

Lower your eyes and focus about a metre (three feet) in front of you.

Rest your hands gently on your knees.

2 Breathe normally through your nose, using your abdomen rather than your chest.

Check your posture and relax any part of your body that is tense.

3 Begin counting your breath and when you reach ten begin again.

When thoughts intervene label them as 'thinking' and return to concentrate on your breath.

4 Meditate in this way for about ten minutes. Try this meditation for a week.

See if you notice how changeable and ephemeral your thoughts are.

SPACIOUS MIND

With one thought constantly following another, your mind may start to feel claustrophobic.

This meditation will help you clear your mental 'space' and give you a much-needed mental holiday.

Any time you are feeling stressed and hemmed in by worries or constant thinking, use this meditation.

1 Sit crossed-legged on a cushion or a straight-backed chair with your feet flat on the floor.

2 Begin by focusing on your breath, counting on the out-breath up to ten.

  After about five minutes, stop counting your breath and simply focus on the out-breath for another two minutes or so.

3 Become aware of the calmness and space that arises at the end of the out-breath.

  Let yourself float deeper and deeper into that feeling and space.

  Imagine your breath flowing out into a vast area filled with light.

4 With each breath, let the space get larger and larger.

  Allow yourself to rest and be in that space in the present.

  If a thought appears, gently refocus on the spaciousness you have created.

5 Tell yourself that it is okay to just be. Remain in this calm space as long as you like.

  When you are ready, take a deep breath and end your session.

DISTRACTED MIND

When meditating on the breath, thoughts can pull
us off track. But distractions can originate outside
ourselves in the form of sounds, lights or smells.
Labelling them helps you return to focusing on
your breath.

Try this variation for ten minutes, both morning and evening.

1 Sit cross-legged on a cushion with your bottom slightly raised. If you can't sit cross-legged, sit on a chair.

   Keep your back straight, your shoulders level and relaxed and your chin parallel to the floor.

   Lower your eyes and focus about a metre (three feet) in front of you. Rest your hands gently on your knees.

2 Breathe normally through your nose, using your abdomen rather than your chest. Check your posture and relax any part of your body that is tense.

3 Begin counting your breath on each exhalation and when you reach ten, begin again.

   Notice if you are distracted by anything external such as the sound of a car starting, cooking smells from next door or changes in the light or temperature in your room.

   Label the distraction and return to focusing on your breath.

4 Keep track of any distractions you encounter for a week.

   Notice if your reaction to external distraction differs from internal thought distraction.

   Notice if your irritation lessens over time.

NINE-ROUND BREATHING

This is a Tibetan Buddhist breathing and purification practice, useful for balancing your mind and reducing negative thoughts before any meditation session.

Practise before any meditation session or when you want to reduce negative emotions.

1 Visualize your body as completely empty and transparent.

During the first round of breathing, inhale through your left nostril keeping the right closed with your left index finger.

Imagine breathing in and filling your body with pure white light. While exhaling, imagine that any obsessions with sex or material possessions leave via your right nostril in the form of black smoke.

Repeat three times.

2 Hold your left nostril closed with your right index finger and inhale pure white light through your right nostril.

You are now clearing your anger and hatred, which leave via your left nostril in the form of black smoke.

Repeat three times.

3 Breathe in white light through both nostrils. Breathe out any ignorance or mental confusion in the form of black smoke.

Imagine this smoke leaving your body at the point between your eyebrows, which meditation masters refer to as your third eye or wisdom eye.

Repeat three times.

4 From this calm, centred and purified state, begin the meditation practice of your choice.

DANCING FLAME

A single candle flame is a wonderful object on which to focus your mind. It draws your attention and its warmth, light and beauty are timeless and reassuring.

Try this meditation at night whenever you are feeling overwhelmed and fearful about some aspect of your life.

1 Sit on a cushion or chair about a metre (three feet) away from your candle, which should be at eye level. Other lighting in the room should be low but not absent. Try to eliminate any draughts.

2 Begin your session with Nine-round breathing (following the instructions from that section of this chapter).

3 Focus on the candle flame and try to empty your mind of all thoughts. With each in-breath, allow the light and warmth of the candle flame to free your mind of any fears, anxiety or insecurity.

When extraneous thoughts intervene, refocus on the candle flame in front of you.

4 Meditate in this way for ten to fifteen minutes.

LIVING MINDFULLY

GLASS HALF-FULL

It is easy to take what you have for granted and be chronically dissatisfied. Focusing on what blessings you have can transform your mind and your life.

If you are preoccupied with wanting things you don't have.

1 Write down everything you want that you don't have.
Then write down ten things for which you are grateful.

2 Find time to be alone in a place where you will not be
disturbed. Sit in any way that makes you comfortable.
After doing the preliminary exercise above, read over the
ten things that you have listed.

3 Generate a sincere sense of gratitude for each item on
your list.

If you are grateful for your health, feel thankful for your
good fortune. If you have a car, no matter what condition,
be sincerely grateful to have transportation. If you have a
partner, think of their wonderful qualities and be grateful
that they are a part of your life.

4 After you have gone through your list, sit quietly and thank
yourself, God, the universe, or whomever or whatever you
choose, for the gifts you have been given. Resolve, on
a daily basis, to be mindful and grateful for the blessings
you have.

MONKEY MIND

While you are awake, you are thinking constantly.
Your mind may jump from one thought to another,
like a monkey leaping from branch to branch. This
meditation helps you to be more mindful of what you
are thinking.

This meditation helps when you are chronically distracted, feeling scattered in your thinking or having difficulty concentrating.

1 Take a few deep breaths to signal that you are going to focus on this meditation. Immediately begin to watch your thoughts. Notice how quickly and seamlessly your mind jumps from one idea, impression and thought to another.

2 Think back to a few minutes ago and try to remember what you were thinking. Trace how you got to what you are thinking now.

3 Look at a watch or a clock for 60 seconds. Make hash marks with a pencil every time your thoughts change during the minute.

4 Bring this new awareness into your daily life. Try to be more mindful of what you are thinking, rather than getting lost in thought.

WHAT ARE YOU THINKING?

Noting the content of your thoughts when you meditate on your breath will help you to discover patterns in your thinking and be more mindful of your thought processes.

Try this for ten minutes, morning and evening.

1 Sit cross-legged on a cushion with your bottom slightly raised. If you can't sit cross-legged, sit on a chair.

Keep your back straight, your shoulders level and relaxed and your chin parallel to the floor.

Lower your eyes and focus about a metre (three feet) in front of you. Rest your hands gently on your knees.

2 Breathe normally through your nose, using your abdomen rather than your chest. Check your posture and relax any part of your body that is tense.

3 Begin counting your breath and when you reach ten, begin again. When thoughts intervene, note the content. For instance, if you thought about money problems, silently note 'worrying about money' and return to counting your breath.

4 Meditate for about ten minutes. At the end of your session write down which thoughts emerged. Do this for one week and notice any recurring patterns. Notice if your thoughts about something or someone change over the week.

YOU HAVE A BODY

Meditating on mindfulness of physical sensations allows you to become more aware of your body. If you have been split off mentally from your body, this meditation will help you reconnect your mind with your physical self.

Try this mindfulness meditation whenever you are feeling disconnected from your body.

1 Sit on a cushion or a chair keeping your back as straight as possible, yet relaxed. Calm your mind by observing your breath.

2 Shift the focus on your breath to another part of your body. Choose a spot that is easy to feel, like your neck or your knee. Focus all your awareness on that spot. Try to merge with any sensations you may feel.

Observe the sensation without judging it as pleasant or unpleasant.

3 Is the sensation a tightness, a burning or a tingling? Is it a combination of many sensations? Do they change over time? Keep your awareness on the spot. If thoughts intrude, return your focus to the spot you have chosen.

4 If you want, switch to another part of your body and repeat the same exercise. When ready, end your meditation. Try to bring this mindfulness of your body into your daily life.

DO I HAVE AN ATTITUDE?

Your attitude towards anyone or anything you
encounter is usually one of either attraction, aversion
or indifference. Using meditation to become aware
of your attitudes leads you to greater mental balance
and stability.

Try this meditation when you are feeling particularly judgemental or self-centred in your dealings with others.

1 Find a quiet place indoors where you can be alone. Sit on a cushion or on a straight-backed chair. Choose one object, a situation or a person on which to focus for this meditation session. Mentally take time to create a vivid and detailed image of your chosen object.

2 As you meditate, allow your feelings to arise and carefully note your attitude. Don't suppress a negative attitude or edit it to what you think you should feel. Accept without judgement any attitude you may have.

3 Ask yourself a series of questions to explore your attitude more closely. Have you always felt this way towards this object or person?

What led to you feeling this way? What could cause your attitude to change? Note any bodily sensations that arise.

4 As you deepen your understanding of your attitude, remind yourself that what you feel is only what you feel today. Try to cultivate an attitude of equanimity; that is, not feeling any judgement at all. Remind yourself that attitudes, like everything else, change over time.

AUTUMN LEAF

To perceive without bias or judgement is a difficult
task for anyone. Unfortunately, labelling and
judgements prevent you from experiencing life
directly. This simple awareness meditation will help
you to experience nature more deeply and joyfully.

Practise this meditation when you feel separated from
nature and distanced from your own direct experience
of life.

1 Walk for a few minutes in the park or woods while focusing
on your breath. Try to empty your mind of all thoughts.

2 Stop walking, pick up a fallen leaf and hold it in your
hand. Notice if you are judging the leaf in any way – for
its appearance, size or colour, or if you are comparing it to
another you didn't pick up. Try to let go of any thoughts or
judgements about the leaf.

3 Begin by simply taking in the leaf visually as if you were a
Martian and had never seen one before. Notice its exquisite
shape, colour and the tiny delicate veins spreading from its
centre. If it has blemishes from insects or decay, see them
as equally beautiful and perfect.

4 Spend time being with the leaf in this way. Try to bring this
way of experiencing the leaf to the rest of your life. Notice
if you feel more relaxed, more fulfilled and more aware of
the beauty all around you.

HEALING BODY, MIND & SPIRIT

PURIFYING FIRE

If you have bad habits that affect your mental, emotional, physical or spiritual health, this meditation will help you let go of them and start anew.

Healing is not just for physical illness. Try this when you are struggling with negative habits.

1 Write down any negative habits you have had in the past or have presently. Take your time and be as thorough as possible. Then write down any feelings you have about your negative habits. Include any shame or regret.

2 Build a fire in your fireplace or barbecue. Sit on a meditation cushion or a chair nearby. Read your list. Review everything and feel your shame and regret.

3 Visualize your higher power in any form you like. Express your regret for indulging in negative habits and ask for help in living your life in a more positive and constructive way. Feel your higher power's love and acceptance of you as you are.

4 Now place your list into the fire and watch it burn. As your list burns, visualize your negative habits leaving you. Let go of any shame by mentally giving it to the fire to be purified. Commit to living a more positive life.

49 DAYS

Tibetan Buddhists believe in reincarnation. When someone dies, it is understood he or she will spend up to 49 days in transit to the next life. During this time you grieve for them and also pray that they have a good rebirth.

Practise this meditation during and up to 49 days after the death of a loved one.

1 Sit on a cushion or chair in front of a table on which you have placed the photograph of your loved one.

2 Think of your loved one and let your grief pour out. Cry as much as you need to. Express how much you appreciated them and will miss them. When you can, begin to think about their spirit and affirm to yourself that he or she will live on in some form.

3 If you believe in reincarnation, imagine your loved one taking a wonderful rebirth. Pray that the person will have a good new life where he or she will continue to progress on a spiritual path. Mentally release your loved one to a new life. If you feel that the person will be in heaven with God, visualize the person there.

4 If you don't believe in an afterlife, remember the good aspects of your departed loved one and visualize letting him or her go. Release yourself from any guilt or sadness. Visualize your loved one's best quality and bring that quality into your life as a way to remember him or her.

TAP AWAY

There are many new therapeutic techniques for dealing with stress based on tapping opposite sides of your body. This one is simple and forms the basis of a powerful meditation.

Practise this technique whenever you are suffering anxiety caused by something in your past or something you are currently worried about.

1 Sit in a straight-backed chair with your back straight and your hands resting on your thighs.

2 Think about the cause of your anxiety. Visualize as clearly as possible the event, people or situation and fully feel your distress.

3 Now using your index finger, begin to tap lightly, first on one thigh then the other, alternating back and forth. Do this rhythmically, at a speed that feels comfortable to you, and that you can sustain for three minutes or more. As you tap, keep visualizing the source of your stress.

4 After three minutes you should feel a lessening of your anxiety. If the anxiety is still partially there, repeat the exercise another time. If it is not completely gone after the second exercise, try again, only this time move your eyes from side to side.

FEED YOUR DEMONS

If you suffer from addictions – drugs, alcohol,
food, sex, Internet or whatever – you are probably
running away from pain and not nurturing yourself in
appropriate ways. Try this meditation to learn how to
take better care of yourself.

Try this meditation to begin healing from your troublesome addictions.

1 Sit on a cushion or straight-backed chair in a quiet, private place.

2 Bring to mind what you consider to be your most troublesome addiction. Now see your addiction as a person other than yourself. For instance, if your addiction is to cigarettes, you might see your addiction as a thin, sallow-skinned man who is tense and hunched over.

3 Ask the person you have created what he is feeling and what he needs that he is not getting. Your smoking character might tell you he wants to relax, clear his lungs and quit racing around all the time.

4 After you have had a conversation with your 'demon' imagine you are responsible for their care and visualize helping them heal. Think of at least one way you could help them feel better and stop abusing themselves. Now apply this nurturing solution to your own life.

HOLD THE OPPOSITES

You may find yourself locked into dualistic thinking
– everything has to be right or wrong, black or white,
good or bad. This meditation helps you learn to
tolerate a more realistic view of life.

If you find yourself angry and fearful, wanting simplistic, clear answers or demanding that things be done 'your way', try this meditation to help you tolerate life as it really is.

1 Sit on a cushion or straight-backed chair in a quiet place where you can be alone. Meditate by watching your breath for about five minutes.

2 Think of a situation where you have been miserable because you wanted something to be a certain way and the other person wanted another outcome. Pay attention to your emotions. The first one to arise may be anger. Check to see if underneath the anger you feel fear. What will you lose if you let both points of view exist simultaneously?

3 Imagine that you are alone on a desert island with that person and your survival depends on both of you having your needs met. Imagine a creative way to compromise so that each of you has at least part of what you desire.

4 After you have reached your compromise solution whereby both you and the other person can be 'right' and have something of what you want, notice if you feel less stress and more contentment.

NECTAR WASHING

Visualization is a powerful tool for healing body, mind and spirit. Use this meditation to ward off illness.

Try this meditation if you are ill. This is also a wonderful meditation to practise on a regular basis for maintaining your good general health.

1 Sit down for a few minutes and write down any health problems you have, however small or serious. Now sit on a cushion or chair in your usual meditation space. Begin watching your breath for a few minutes.

2 Think of all the health problems you listed. See them as black spots residing in various parts of your body. Note how your health problems hinder your life, feel any emotions that arise.

3 Visualize that you are near a beautiful waterfall in a warm, tropical location. No one is around. Undress and find a place where you can sit directly under the flow. Imagine that the water is not ordinary water, but a heavenly nectar that heals illness and prevents disease.

4 Visualize all your health problems being cleansed by this nectar. Feel the nectar not only flowing over your body but through it as well, taking with it all the black spots you visualized earlier.

5 Affirm to yourself that your body is now free of health problems. Get up from your seat under the waterfall, dry off and put on your clothes. Leave this beautiful site knowing that you are in vibrant health. Know that you can return to it whenever you want.

GET MOVING

RUNNER'S WAY

If you are a runner, you may have already experienced
a meditative state while running. Use this meditation
to make it more focused and conscious.

Meditate whenever you run by yourself.

1 Begin meditating as you put on your T-shirt, shorts and running shoes. Do this mindfully, focusing on each task.

2 As you begin running, meditate as you would for 'Watching Your Breath' (see Calming and Centring section) except you are moving instead of sitting down on a cushion or chair.

3 Now let go of your concentration on your breath, and focus on the act of running. Try not to let thoughts enter your mind; when they do, simply return your focus to running. Begin to feel your body, mind and soul functioning together as one. Continue to stay in the present moment, very much aware of everything around you.

4 When you finish your run, take off your shoes and socks and stand on the grass. Feel connected to the Earth and grounded in your body. Continue to be mindful of the present throughout your day.

WEEDING

If you are a gardener, you understand weeding. Why not make your weeding into a meditative practice? If you don't have a garden, offer to weed for someone else or volunteer with your local parks service.

Try this meditation when doing some gardening.

1 Sit quietly under a tree. Bring to mind any negative habits you may have, such as a bad temper or procrastinaton. Think of as many as you like. Visualize the weeds in the patch as your negative habits.

2 Get up from under the tree and approach the area you are planning to weed. See that whole area as you or your mind. See the flowers and plants as your positive traits and the weeds as those negative traits that you would like to eliminate.

3 As you begin to weed, try to stay very focused and mindful. When you pull out a weed by its roots, think that you are pulling out your own negative habit by the roots. Continue in this way until all the weeds are removed.

4 Finish by cultivating, feeding and watering the plants and flowers. Think of them as your positive traits that you would like to nurture.

WALKING ZEN

Zen Buddhists practise a wonderful walking meditation called *kinhin*. You do not have to be a Buddhist to enjoy this calming, centring, mindful and moving meditation.

Try this when you want to slow down and be more precise in your work or your relationships.

1 Mark out a route beforehand. You can do walking meditation indoors by circling around a room or by walking outdoors in your garden or along a path. If outdoors, it should be where you can be alone.

2 Stand with your back straight and try to remain relaxed. Place your hands together just below your sternum or heart, with your left hand in a soft fist, wrapping your fingers lightly around your thumb. Then place your right hand over your left with your right thumb across the top of your left hand. Keep your elbows slightly extended from your sides.

3 Begin walking slowly along the route you decided on in your preparation, either inside or outside. Begin by taking a half-step with every cycle of breath (inhalation and exhalation). So, it is heel first (half-step) and ball of foot (half-step). Your pace will be extremely slow. As you walk, focus on your breath. Keep your eyes lowered and directed straight ahead. Don't look from side to side.

4 Stop. Now switch to a normal walking pace for a few minutes. Keep focusing on your breath. Breathe naturally. End your meditation when you feel ready to do so.

DANCE TRANCE

You can say your prayers, but you can also dance your
prayers. Dance can help you transcend your ordinary
mind and access the Divine. Try this dancing form
of meditation.

If you feel that you are about to explode from stress and unexpressed emotions, try this dancing meditation to help you figure out what is going on.

1 Find time when you can be alone. Go barefoot or wear shoes you can dance in comfortably. Wear clothes that are very loose and free. Take off your glasses and wristwatch. Now clear the area in which you are going to dance.

2 Put on some music and turn it up as loud as possible. Begin dancing and don't stop for 30 minutes. If you want to keep dancing for longer, do so.

3 While you are dancing try to focus on your dance. Try not to think and carry on dancing until you are exhausted. Try to feel connected to your higher power as you dance. If you feel emotional or feel like crying, don't hold back.

4 When you feel that you have danced as much as you can, end your dance meditation.

WHIRLING DERVISH

Sufis practise whirling or spinning to get in touch
with the Divine. Accompany your whirling with
trance-like music and see what happens and how it
makes you feel.

Try whirling as a form of meditation when you are open to having an ecstatic connection with the Divine.

1 Start playing a CD of instrumental music. Stretch your right arm out in front of your body, with the palm of your hand facing your heart. Extend your left arm up towards heaven.

2 Fix your gaze on the hand in front of you and begin turning slowly clockwise. If it feels better to turn anticlockwise, reverse your hand positions. It is said that turning anticlockwise feels more inward and clockwise more outward.

3 If you should start to feel dizzy, simply slow down. Try pivoting on your heel, then the ball of your foot to see what works best for you.Rotate your head while you whirl.

4 To end your whirling meditation, slow down gradually and stop. Stand quietly for a few moments.

SUN SALUTATION

This famous yoga asana, surya-namaskar, will get you moving early in the day. Practise this as a meditation first thing in the morning to engender a sense of gratitude and purpose.

Practise sun salutation in the morning.

1   Stand with your feet hip-width apart, hands by your sides.
    Inhale, raise your arms overhead and arch back as far as
    feels comfortable.

2   As you exhale, bend forward and rest your hands beside
    your feet. Inhale and step the right leg back with hands
    still on the floor.

3   Exhale and step the left leg back. Now you are in a push-up
    position with arms fully extended. Hold the position and
    inhale. Exhale and lower yourself as if coming down from
    a push-up. Only your hands and feet should touch the floor.

4   Inhale and stretch forward and up, bending at the waist.
    Use your arms to lift your torso, but only bend back as far
    as is comfortable.

    Exhale, lift and push your hips back and up with your head
    facing down between your straight legs.

5   Inhale and step your right foot forward. Exhale, bring your
    left foot forward and pull your head to your knees. Inhale
    and stand tall while keeping your arms extended over your
    head. Exhale and lower your arms to your sides. Repeat the
    sequence, stepping back with the left leg first.

LOVE &
COMPASSION

TONGLEN FOR YOURSELF

Tonglen is a Tibetan Buddhist practice for developing compassion. In the *tonglen* visualization, you receive, with an open heart, the suffering of others and give selflessly all of your love, joy and well-being to them. It is best to practise *tonglen* for yourself first.

Practise *tonglen* for yourself when you are having difficulties or problems with chronic self-hatred. You can practise this meditation at any time, anywhere.

1 For formal practice, sit in meditation posture on your cushion or chair in a quiet place. Or you can practise whenever and wherever you like.

2 Focus on any difficulties you are currently experiencing. If you are sad and regretful or if you are stressed out about money, bring that problem to your full awareness.

3 Breathe your problems and difficulties into your heart. Visualize your difficulties being dissolved and transformed. Now see them ride out on your out-breath as happiness and joy, luminosity and fearlessness.

4 Practise *tonglen* with the hope of healing your attitude and restoring yourself to wholeness. Continue exhaling and inhaling, riding your breath in this way for as long as you like.

TONGLEN FOR OTHERS

After practising *tonglen* meditation for yourself, this *tonglen* meditation will teach you how to practise it in order to develop feelings of compassion for others.

Practise *tonglen* for those close to you when you become aware that they are suffering.

1 Sit in meditation posture on your chair or practise spontaneously any time and anywhere you want. Breathe for a few minutes to calm your mind. Then imagine having unlimited love and compassion.

2 Think of someone close to you, who you know is suffering from life problems or illness. Visualize the person in front of you.

3 Breathe in their suffering in the form of black smoke and let it gather in your heart. Be willing to take it on and remove it from them. As it reaches your heart imagine it dissolving all your self-centredness. Now breathe out love, joy and compassion. Don't hold anything back.

4 When you first start this practice, you may have some difficulty visualizing taking in other peoples' suffering and giving away all your joy and happiness to them. But over time, this will change. You will discover that you have an abundance of positive resources, more than you can imagine.

5 Continue taking and sending on your breath for as long as you like. End when you are ready.

REPAYING KINDNESS

This is a wonderful meditation for realizing
the kindness of others. It will help you develop
compassion and reduce any self-centredness that may
creep into your thoughts.

Try this meditation when you are feeling alone
and struggling.

1 Begin by making a list of everyone who took care of you as
a child. Sit on your cushion or straight-backed chair. Light
a candle in memory of all those who have helped you in
your life.

2 Recall the list you made in preparation for your meditation.
Begin with your mother and father; then go on to siblings,
aunts and uncles, grandparents and cousins, all of whom
cared for you in some way. Then think of your teachers,
your babysitters, clergy, coaches and friends. Think of your
first job and the person who hired you. Now consider the
farmers who grew the food you ate and the shops that sold
the food. Return to your parents who worked hard for you
to have a home, clothes, food, schooling and medical care.
Think of your doctors and dentists. Your list is merely the
tip of the iceberg.

3 Continue to add to your list. Generate a sincere sense of
gratitude to every person who has helped you in your life.
Realize you have been the recipient of so much kindness it
will take lifetimes to repay everyone. Vow to pay back all of
that kindness by generating love and compassion for them
and for all beings.

FREE SENTIENT BEINGS

This practice helps you to generate more compassion
for all non-human sentient beings, including animals,
birds, insects and fish. In this meditation, you free
animals, birds, fish or insects that might otherwise
be killed.

Try doing this meditation practice as a ritual once a year.

1 Find an animal, an injured bird, a fish or an insect that you can release safely into the wild. Make sure it is in the best interest of the being you are releasing. You can find good subjects in a fisherman's bait shop, such as worms or tiny fish compatible with your local environment.

2 Take your animal, bird, fish or insects to the place where you will release them.

3 Stand or sit comfortably and focus on your breath for a few minutes to centre yourself.

4 Think for a moment of all suffering beings in the animal realm. Visualize the difficulties of their lives on a day-to-day basis. Wish for the small beings you are about to release and all others in the animal realm to have happiness and be free from suffering. With that sincere wish, release them into the wild.

LOVE YOURSELF

Self-hatred is common in our culture. This meditation
will help you counteract any feelings of self-hatred,
including shame or low self-esteem.

Try this meditation when you become aware of self-hatred.

1 Sit on a cushion or chair in a quiet place. Visualize your higher power sitting in front of you. It could be Jesus, Buddha, Shakti, Mohammed or just a wise form of your self.

2 Imagine your higher power smiling at you with great love and compassion, accepting you as you are. Understand that he or she does not demand that you 'fix' anything about yourself to deserve his or her love. Know that he or she wants you to accept yourself exactly as you are, and treat yourself with kindness and respect as they already do.

3 Thank your higher power for reminding you to be kind towards yourself. Tell him or her that with their help and encouragement, you will refrain from hating yourself and will encourage yourself to accept yourself exactly as you are. Promise that you will try to live your life with complete self-acceptance and self-love.

UNCONDITIONAL LOVE

Most often our love is conditional – based on whether our loved ones behave the way we would like or support us in our endeavours. But a better love is one without conditions – we love them as they are, regardless of what they do.

Practise this meditation if you have control issues in your relationships.

1 Sit on a cushion or chair in your private meditation space. Begin by watching your breath and calming body and mind.

2 Bring to mind your partner or other loved one. List any conditions you have that limit your love for them. For example, you may find you love them on condition that they make a lot of money, buy you flowers for special events or wear certain clothes. Note how these conditions, while seeming rational, constrict your heart. Note how this doesn't sound like love, more like a demand that your needs be met.

3 Now visualize giving your loved one complete freedom to be and do what they want. Does this frighten you, make you sad or change how you feel about them? Bring to mind the qualities you love about this person. Perhaps you love their energy, their courage and their ability to respond to others.

4 Imagine them not being with you or available to meet your needs and loving them anyway. Feel your heart expand as you accept and love them wholeheartedly, regardless of what they do or don't do.

BROTHERS & SISTERS

All religions encourage you to love your parents,
but many do not say as much about siblings. Try
this meditation to heal your sibling relationship and
encourage love between you.

This is a great meditation to practise before a family holiday or event.

1 Sit on your cushion or chair in your meditation space. Place some photos of your siblings on a table in front of you. Light a candle. Meditate on your breath for a few minutes. Now call on your higher power to sit alongside you. Introduce him or her to your siblings.

2 Let any feelings emerge. Ask your higher power to help you heal your relationships, if they need healing. If they don't, ask that your relationships deepen and strengthen over your lifetimes. If you have unproductive ways of relating that are rooted in your childhood, ask that you be able to shed them and find a new, more mature model.

3 Now recall the positive qualities in each of your brothers and sisters. Ask that you be able to accept and love them exactly as they are.

4 Close your meditation by committing to honour and respect each of your siblings and strengthen the relationships you have with them.

PROBLEM
SOLVING

YOU CAN LET GO NOW

Do you have control issues? Has anyone told you that you are controlling? This meditation will help you learn to let go.

If you have received any complaints about your controlling behaviour, you might want to try this meditation.

1 Write about three occasions on which you can remember feeling anxiety and wanting to control someone else's behaviour, even if it seemed justified to you at the time. Sit on a cushion or chair in your meditation space. Watch your breath for five minutes.

2 Choose one of the events you listed. Try to recall it in detail. Feel what you were feeling at the time. Perhaps your partner moved a chair and didn't move it back to where you had placed it when he or she left the room. Was your first feeling one of anger?

3 Ask yourself why it is so important to have things the way you want them, especially since you are sharing your life with another person. If you weren't feeling anger, would you feel fear? Are you afraid something may happen unexpectedly and you will feel powerless, alone, abandoned? Explore the fear behind your need to control.

4 Commit to letting go a little at a time on a daily basis by looking for the fear behind the need for you to control. Relax your grip on things and notice that usually nothing terrible happens. Be kind and patient with yourself in this process.

HIGH ROAD

If you are facing a difficult decision, where 'doing the right thing' may have negative consequences, it may be hard to follow your moral and ethical principles. This meditation will help you take the 'high road' if that is what you choose to do.

Try this meditation to help you live according to your values.

1 Sit on a cushion or chair and meditate by watching your breath for five minutes.

2 Bring to mind the situation that is troubling you. If there were no negative consequences, what would you do? What action would feel most congruent with your values? Visualize yourself talking to whomever you need to and taking any action you feel appropriate.

3 Visualize the same situation, but this time bring to mind any negative consequences that may come your way if you do what you feel is right. Imagine how you will feel if you lost your job or your friend? Would you feel more comfortable if you acted in line with how you would like to live your life? Would acting on your principles help some and harm others?

4 Sometimes there are no black or white answers, but spending time quietly trying out ethical decisions is the best way to come to know what is best. Ask your higher power to help you make the most compassionate decision for yourself and anyone else involved.

MAKE PEACE WITH MONEY

Money – making it, having it, wanting it – is central to
most people's lives and a source of great anxiety for
many. This meditation helps you make peace
with money.

Try this meditation if you are obsessed with thinking about money.

1 Write about what money means to you and what role it plays in your life. Sit on a cushion or straight-backed chair in your private meditation space. Breathe deeply for a few minutes to clear your mind.

2 Review what you wrote down and put it aside. Explore how you feel when you have money. Do you feel more real or substantial? Do you feel you exist more solidly than when you don't have money?

3 Now imagine how you feel when you are broke. Are you diminished, deflated and less valuable? Notice you don't become more solid or less substantial when you have or don't have money. Contemplate how money functions as an idea, causing you to feel more or less valuable.

4 Contemplate ten things that are not measured in monetary terms, such as the loving gaze of your partner, a wonderful conversation with a friend, the laughter of your child or the playfulness of your pet.

5 End your meditation by affirming that you are valuable with or without money. Commit to meditating on the meaning of money to help you counteract the cultural message of materialism. Seek out and value those precious experiences money can't buy.

GET OUT OF DEBT

The habit of living beyond your means may be
dragging you down mentally, physically and
spiritually. This meditation will help you to find the
courage to get yourself out of debt.

If you have a problem with credit-card debt, practise this meditation on a weekly basis until you are out of debt.

1 Sit on a cushion or chair in your meditation space. Light a candle to help you focus.

2 Gather your records together and add up how much you are in debt. Say the amount out loud: 'I am [however much] in debt'. Let that fact resonate in your consciousness. How do you feel saying that fact out loud? If you feel numb or if you feel fear, anxiety or shame, note it. How does your body feel when you say the amount out loud? Do you experience a feeling of tension or is your breathing constricted?

3 After admitting to yourself the extent of your debt, generate a sense of compassion for your difficulties in controlling your spending. From this place of compassion commit to getting out of debt, no matter how long it takes. Ask your higher power to help you control your spending and give you the courage to seek professional help if you need it.

4 End your meditation by making a promise to your higher power that you will stop spending on credit and will reduce the amount you owe every month by paying off some of the balance.

WORKAHOLISM

What used to be called 'workaholism' is fast becoming the norm for white collar workers. Long hours and taking work home is expected if you want to compete in the corporate world. This meditation helps you to find a better alternative.

Try this meditation if you are questioning your fast-paced lifestyle.

1 Start by writing down your typical schedule for a week. Sit on a cushion or chair in your meditation space. Meditate by watching your breath for five minutes.

2 Look over your schedule. How much time did you spend with your loved ones or friends? Did you get eight hours' sleep a night? When did you relax and play during the week? Did you eat well and exercise? Did you tend to your spiritual life? Are you using your hectic schedule to avoid intimacy? How much money are you really making an hour?

3 Now contemplate your long-term goals. What do you want to achieve? When you are on your deathbed, how do you want to have spent your life?

4 Think about the qualities you would like to manifest in your life. Do you want warmth, love, fun, play, spiritual development and time in nature? How is your current life helping you have this quality of life?

5 End your meditation by affirming what is most important to you and committing to creating a more balanced life.

FACING THE MIRROR

Everyone has difficulties and problems that persist over time. You are not alone in this. It is time to face your problems directly, with courage and honesty.

Try this meditation when you feel you are avoiding your problems.

1 Find a time when you can be alone. Stand in front of your bathroom mirror or a full-length mirror.

2 Look at your reflection. Speaking out loud, tell yourself three things you like about yourself. It could be that you are a good listener, a very intelligent person or a great cook. Love the person looking back at you. Tell yourself you know you are struggling, but it is important to admit to the problem that has been dragging you down.

3 Out loud, in a clear voice, tell yourself the problem you have been avoiding. For example, you might say 'I am overweight and I need to lose it for my health and well-being'. Repeat your statement three times.

4 Now commit to taking a step to resolve your problem within the next 24 hours. Say out loud what you plan to do. Repeat it three times.

5 Close your meditation by congratulating yourself for your courage and honesty.

MANIFESTING YOUR DREAMS & CONNECTING TO THE DIVINE

FOR THE HIGHEST GOOD

If you have a dream – to start a business, build a house, write a book – manifest your dream, not just for yourself, but for the highest good of all.

Try this meditation if you want to start a project or manifest a dream.

1 Sit on a cushion or chair in your meditation space and light a candle. Invite your higher power to join you in this meditation and guide you in your effort to manifest whatever you wish, however small or significant.

2 Think of what it is you would like to manifest. Ask your higher power that this thing, or relationship, or project be for the benefit of all beings, including yourself. Ask that this selfless motivation may guide all your decisions and activities regarding the project.

3 Visualize that your dream has manifested. What would it look like? How would it feel? If it is a business, see yourself in your office having a meeting with your employees. If you want to run for office, envision yourself giving a campaign speech. Now that it is a reality, is your dream in line with your highest ideals and for the benefit of all?

4 If your dream is indeed for the highest good of all, and you want it to become a reality, write it down and place it in a silver box. Ask your higher power to help you make it a reality.

SOUL WORK

What is it that you are meant to do in this lifetime?
What is your special contribution?
Try a little soul work to explore these very
important questions.

Practise this meditation if you feel you are at a crossroads in your life and need to do something new.

1 Consider then write down what you care about most deeply and what excites you most intensely.

2 Sit on a cushion or chair in your meditation space. Light a candle and incense to affirm the importance of this moment and the sacredness of your life. Meditate by watching your breath for a few minutes in order to calm your mind and relax your body.

3 Read out loud what you wrote in preparation for this meditation. You may have written that you care most about your family, world peace or the environment. Perhaps science lights a fire in your soul. Let yourself feel any emotions that arise. Are you excited, sad, angry? Did you let your family talk you out of taking a certain job because it didn't have the prestige they felt you should aspire to? Do you spend enough time with your loved ones?

4 Contemplate how you are living your life today and whether it honours what you have written in your statement. There is no fault here, just awareness. Knowing what you care about and what excites you will start you on the path to a more fulfilled life.

SPIRIT OF PLACE

Are you happy where you are living? Would another location suit you better? This meditation helps you explore the right location for you – body and spirit.

Try this meditation if you want to feel more connected to where you live.

1 Stretch out on a mat on the floor and make yourself comfortable. Cover yourself with a blanket if you need to. Breathe deeply for a few minutes and relax all your muscles from your toes to your crown.

2 Visualize your ideal place to live. Describe the town or city or countryside. Is it a large urban area or a small town? Is it in the country in which you now live or somewhere else in the world? What do the buildings look like?

3 Now describe the weather. Is your ideal place in a warmer climate, a temperate one or in a colder region? Imagine yourself dressed appropriately in this place. Describe the people who live in your ideal place. Are they older, younger, progressive, conservative or intellectuals?

4 What sort of house are you living in? Is it large, small, picturesque, cosy, impressive or modest? Who are you living with? Why does this place nurture your body and soul?

5 If you already live in your ideal place, feel grateful for that fact. If you would like to move somewhere else, repeat this meditation until you find your place of spirit.

SOUL MATE

A soul mate can be your spouse or a friend. It is someone you love deeply, who shares your spiritual journey.

If you want to attract a soul mate, practise this meditation for 30 days.

1 Stretch out on a mat on the floor. Make yourself comfortable, breathe deeply and relax fully.

2 Review the main points of your spiritual autobiography in your mind. Concentrate on where you are now on your spiritual path. What do you believe is your spiritual path and what spiritual work do you envisage for yourself now and in the future?

3 Visualize meeting your soul mate. Are they male or female? What do they look like and what qualities do they possess? Are they sensitive, intelligent, uplifting, generous?

4 Imagine that you have known him or her for lifetimes. Understand this is a reunion rather than a first meeting. Know the person is your spiritual partner, engaged in the same spiritual labour as yourself. Imagine each of you supporting the other as you fulfill your spiritual destiny. Feel blessed to have someone who is a friend whom you trust and who trusts you, with whom you share a true commitment to spiritual work, as well as tenderness and devotion.

5 End your meditation by asking your higher power to help you meet this person in the near future.

MAKE THE LEAP

You may want to manifest your dreams, but fear may be holding you back. Try this meditation to help you take the leap and make your vision a reality.

Try this meditation if you feel ready to manifest a dream, but are afraid to move forward.

1   Sit on a cushion or chair in your meditation space. Meditate by watching your breath for five minutes.

2   Bring to mind a dream you would like to manifest. Ask yourself why you have not moved forward to make it a reality. Explore your beliefs about yourself and how they may be getting in your way.

3   For example, if you have always wanted to learn to ride a horse but are afraid of getting hurt or you feel it is too extravagant for your lifestyle or more fun than you deserve, then examine those beliefs and counter them with new ones. As an example, tell yourself millions of people ride horses without getting hurt, it is money well spent on something that feeds your soul, and of course you deserve to be happy and enjoy your life.

4   End your meditation by committing to take the first step towards making your dream a reality. It may mean a phone call, doing research, signing up for a class or quitting your job. Whatever it is make sure you make the leap into your future and your happiness.

DREAM MAP

Create a dream map for manifesting your dreams.
Then meditate on your map to help your
dreams come true.

Create a dream map when you are ready to act on
your dreams.

1 Find a stack of old magazines, brochures or other visual
material. You will need a base for your map, a plain piece of
paper the size you want your map to be. Then you will need
scissors and glue. If you want to use other art supplies,
gather those as well. Start finding images that symbolize
what you would like to manifest in your life.

2 Find a quiet place where you can be alone. Spread out your
materials on a table or on the floor. Sit quietly for a few
minutes, breathe deeply and open your heart and mind to
your deepest desires. Ask your higher power to help you
manifest dreams that are beneficial not only to you, but to
the rest of the universe.

3 You may want to divide your dream map into areas, such
as spiritual, physical, work, relationships or in any way
that makes sense to you. Begin to arrange and paste down
images that will serve as a reminder of your dreams. Draw,
paint, add glitter or anything else that works for you.

4 When you have finished, ask your higher power to help you
manifest the dreams you have visualized on your dream
map. Place your dream map on a wall where you can see it
every day. If you want to keep it private, put it in a drawer,
but take it out every day, look at it and take action towards
making your dreams come true.

FOUR DIRECTIONS

Many spiritual traditions invoke the four cardinal
directions in their prayers and rituals.

Practise this when you want to ground yourself in your environment.

1 Locate the cardinal directions using your compass. Stand with your spine straight. Take a deep breath. Visualize inhaling your breath into your heart. Exhale very slowly. Feel your heart expand and fill with warmth as you take another deep breath and exhale very slowly. Continue breathing in this way for a few minutes.

2 Now stand facing east. Offer thanks to the east for the water you drink, bathe in and cook with.

3 Rotate to stand facing south. Offer thanks to the south for the Earth and the food you eat.

4 Stand facing west. Offer thanks to the west for fire and the warmth it provides, and its transformative powers.

5 Stand facing north and from your heart, offer thanks to the north for the air you breathe.

6 Now bring your focus to the centre where you are standing. Offer thanks for the environment in which you live. Take a moment to enjoy the state of gratitude you have evoked. Take a deep breath into your heart and exhale.

BUDDHA NATURE

Buddhism teaches that you have Buddha nature.
In other words, you have the capacity to become
enlightened and become a Buddha yourself.

Try this meditation if you are feeling negative about yourself or your potential to develop spiritually.

1 Sit on a cushion or chair in your meditation space. Meditate on your breath for five minutes.

2 Contemplate your own Buddha nature in the form of a seed. Imagine that you begin to 'water' this seed with meditation on patience, love, compassion and other positive topics. Imagine that you strive to be a more positive, loving and compassionate person. Now you have what is called a 'growing Buddha nature'.

3 Over time see yourself slowly eliminating your negative habits and replacing them with positive ones. Imagine your thoughts and actions becoming more positive every day. Imagine how it would be to become a Buddha, to be enlightened.

4 Imagine having no negativity, no suffering and perfect wisdom and compassion. Imagine being able to help all beings. Sit quietly and contemplate what that might be like.

5 If you choose, commit to growing your own Buddha nature by increasing your positive virtues and eliminating your negative habits.

QUAKER WAY

George Fox started the Quaker movement in England in the 17th century. Followers of this movement call themselves 'Friends' or 'Friends of Jesus'.

Try this meditation on a weekly basis with friends or family.

1 Sit facing your friends on chairs or cushions. Together, settle into a quiet space and seek God's presence and will. Let the silence remove any pressure or anxiety you may feel from your daily life. Try to accept yourself exactly as you are and be released from fear, confusion and selfishness. Try to be open to God as well as to each other. Be aware that your intention in listening and waiting in this way is to meet God directly.

2 You may meditate and worship in this way without words, but if you or anyone else present cares to, you can express aloud your experience. Be open and accepting of whatever is said. For example, you may speak about how the teachings of Jesus touch your life or refer to personal experience. Try to receive what others say in a positive way and look for the underlying truth.

3 Contemplate what is essential and eternal rather than trivial. If you speak, express yourself simply and with respect. Look for Truth by sitting quietly and waiting for your heart to open to God's message.

4 End your meditation session whenever your group feels ready.

DEVOTION

There are many spiritual traditions that rely on devotion as a path to spiritual fulfilment. Use this meditation to explore devotion as a direct experience of Divine love.

When you feel your ego is getting in the way of following a spiritual path.

1 Sit on a cushion or chair in your meditation space. Meditate on relinquishing your attachment to superficial concerns that may be getting in the way of your spiritual path. For example, if you are obsessed with clothes and how you look, you may contemplate how this may not be serving you spiritually.

2 Immerse yourself in unselfish, unceasing love for the Divine. On a devotional path everything is an expression of God's love. Your stress, pain and anxiety arise from not seeing the world or yourself as worthy of love. Let go of your ego's painful struggle for recognition and dominance and surrender to Divine love.

3 Imagine every breath you take in is love, and every breath out is compassion. You are an expression of God's love and his or her love flows through you. Consider forming a relationship with a teacher, in whatever form he or she takes. Imagine you are devoted to your teacher and the teachings which empower you to develop on your spiritual path.

4 End your session by meditating on how you might practise devotion in your current spiritual path.

PATH OF GRACE

Grace is at the heart of the Christian tradition. It is God's grace that allows forgiveness and new beginnings. This meditation helps you bring God's grace to your everyday life.

When you want to turn your life around and live in accord with God's grace, as you understand it.

1 Sit on a cushion or chair in your meditation space. Light a candle. Breathe deeply for a few minutes to centre and calm your mind.

2 Contemplate how you can make room for grace in your life. How can you extend the grace you have been given to your family, friends and community? In this world where everything is pushed to its limits and people are emotionally, financially and physically stressed, it is important to help relieve the pressure and create the space for grace to enter. How can you reorganize your priorities so that you can accommodate the needs of your circle for tenderness and grace?

3 Decide on three ways in which you can follow the path of grace. For example, you might invite for dinner a friend with whom you have had a falling-out. Ask your partner how you can be a better partner. Get involved in helping the elderly in your community.

4 End your meditation by composing a prayer to God, thanking Him for all His blessings.

DIVINE FEMININE

The Divine Feminine is an empowering archetype for
both men and women. Meditating on her helps you to
honour all that is feminine in yourself and others.

When you are feeling depressed and suffering
from addictions.

1 Find a quiet place outdoors. Close your eyes and breathe
deeply for a few minutes.

2 Imagine yourself walking along a pathway that leads into
a forest. You come upon a beautiful sanctuary. Slowly you
push open the door and enter. On an altar stands a statue
of the female deity, the Goddess. She does not belong to
any particular religion; she is simply the Mother, God as a
woman, the feminine Divine.

3 As you kneel before her, she begins to teach you about the
sacred feminine and how to honour her. She stresses the
importance of living in the now, the sacredness of your
body and that your being is more important than your
personality. Process, she says, is more important than
product. All matter is sacred and all matter is energy.
Whether you are male or female, your soul is feminine – it
is the receiver of the Divine. Life, death and rebirth are the
natural cycle of existence.

4 Contemplate what she has taught you for as long as you
like. End your meditation by thanking her for her wisdom.
Leave the sanctuary and the forest and return to the place
you chose for meditation.